CHRISTMAS
LOST & FOUND

ALSO BY JOHN A. JENSON

Lost & Found:
Finding the Silver Linings in Life

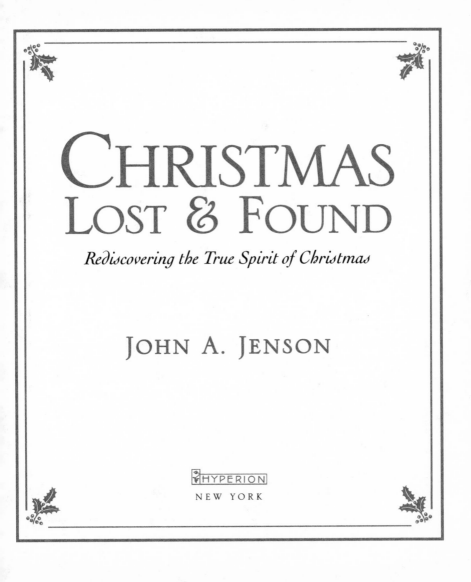

CHRISTMAS
LOST & FOUND

Rediscovering the True Spirit of Christmas

JOHN A. JENSON

HYPERION

NEW YORK

A Special Thanks to Barbara McNichol from Marcom Services for her editing services.

ISBN: 0-7868-6608-X

Designed by Ruth Lee

FIRST EDITION

10 9 8 7 6 5 4 3 2 1

To
My Grandma

who sat by my side
every Christmas Eve for 30 years.
She will always be missed,
and never replaced.

CHRISTMAS
LOST & FOUND

A cold mid-December morning—about what you'd expect in North Dakota. My before-school routine was getting predictable . . . just try to keep warm and inventory my Christmas gifts at the same time.

This morning's ritual, however, was interrupted by my dad who gathered my two brothers and me in the living room to make an announcement. "When you get home from school this afternoon, I may have a surprise for you."

I knew my dad. He never said big things like that, which could only mean one thing. THIS WAS BIG. My pretending-to-be-mature brothers didn't seem quite as excited as I was. But for the first time in a while, I was eager to get to school.

When I arrived at Central Elementary, it didn't take me

long to assemble my fourth-grade buddies and make a declaration of my own. "It appears I'm going to Disney World for Christmas," I announced. The word spread fast, and it was congratulations all around as I began to take addresses from those I thought worthy of receiving a holiday postcard from Florida.

I LOST a lot during that eventful school day—productivity, concentration, and my ability to maintain composure in the wake of such a surprise. I FOUND hope, excitement, and faith that something would happen to bring our family even closer together for the holidays.

—JOHN A. JENSON, 2000

I LOST
sleep as a child wondering
if Santa would appear.

I FOUND,
later in life,
that Santa had been with me day
and night throughout my childhood.

Winning parents don't just show up for the big event.

I LOST
countless hours practicing
"The Little Drummer Boy"
so I could play it just right for my grandma.

I FOUND
that even a poor piano rendition
could bring tears to the eyes of someone
who appreciates the effort.

*Imperfection aimed to please
can be beautiful music to others.*

I LOST

my Christmas cookie privileges when
one showed up crumbled in my bed sheets.

I FOUND

I could have as many as I wanted
until I decided to go undercover.

*Staying on the up-and-up
is the best recipe for maintaining
a full and healthy life.*

I LOST
my reign as "King of the Hill"
after being forcefully pulled from
the top of the icy mound.

I FOUND
it's possible to keep my chin up when
the rest of me is down.

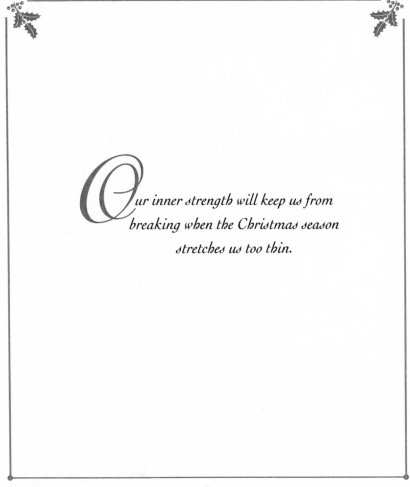

Our inner strength will keep us from breaking when the Christmas season stretches us too thin.

I LOST
faith that Santa would arrive
when my brother pointed out that
we didn't have a chimney.

I FOUND
a father who reassured me of
the ingenuity of old Saint Nick.

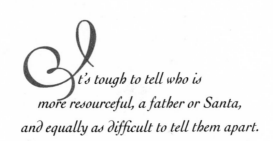

*It's tough to tell who is
more resourceful, a father or Santa,
and equally as difficult to tell them apart.*

I LOST
hours of precious browsing time
when my mom decided to
shop for fabric instead of gifts.

I FOUND
she wasn't trying to frustrate me,
she wanted to make clothes for me.

*Looking after the needs of others is
the common thread that holds
loving families together.*

I LOST

my childlike imagination
when I learned reindeer couldn't fly.

I FOUND

it reappeared while pondering how
they could still bring Christmas to
so many families.

*An eager young mind is
difficult to suppress and
nearly impossible to stop.*

I LOST

my belief in Santa sometime
around the second grade.

I FOUND

the fun in keeping the mystery alive
for those who still waited for him
every Christmas Eve.

Making things happen for others reflects the true spirit of Christmas.

I LOST

the head of my snowman to
the foot of a vandal.

I FOUND

a fresh snowfall helped
restore my creation.

*God will provide us with the elements
to rebuild what man has taken away.*

I LOST

my nerve to ice-skate when
my dad wasn't holding my hand.

I FOUND,

while growing up,
that hand was never very far away.

There are some memories of which we'll never let go.

I LOST
sight of our house every time
I headed down the hill on my sled.

I FOUND
reassurance in seeing my mom
looking out the window every time
I got back to the top.

There is no safer feeling than knowing someone is watching over you.

I LOST
a tooth when I bit into a
rock-hard piece of Christmas candy.

I FOUND,
the next morning,
a quarter tucked neatly beneath my pillow.

*In times of adversity,
it's nice to have faith in something
or someone you can't see or touch.*

I LOST
my cool when my brothers wouldn't stop
messing with my new
Hot Wheels track.

I FOUND,
after my little tantrum,
how quickly my mom could shut down
my entire operation.

*The season of giving is
the wrong time to display selfishness.*

I LOST
trust in Santa
when I realized it was
the man next door wearing the red suit.

I FOUND
that, even though Santa lost some credibility,
my neighbor gained a lot.

*No matter what clothes we wear,
our actions define our character.*

I LOST
my old sledding coat when
my mom gave it to the church.

I FOUND
that the giving of a coat
could warm a heart.

What no longer has value for one person can be priceless to another.

I LOST

my excitement when my mom announced
it would be a slim Christmas for gifts.

I FOUND

that, when all was said and done,
there was nothing meager about it.

*Those wise enough to keep
expectations low have a tendency
to exceed them.*

I LOST

my lines and had to improvise
during the annual Christmas play.

I FOUND

that, though they weren't flawlessly delivered,
the congregation got the message.

*We don't have to be scholars
of the gospel to share the word with others.*

I LOST

appreciation for my classmate
who seemed uninterested in
all the gifts I got for Christmas.

I FOUND

that interest in my good fortune
was not his responsibility.

*We often learn the most
from no reaction at all.*

I LOST
the tiny metal ball that made
the Christmas bell ring.

I FOUND
that little things can really
make a difference.

Appreciating the smallest of contributions
is what makes Christmas
such a big deal.

I LOST

the excitement of receiving new golf clubs
after realizing I couldn't use them
until spring.

I FOUND

that, in four months of visualization,
I never hit a bad shot.

The mind is a wonderful thing
when aimed in the right direction.

I LOST
my traditional spot at the table
when out-of-town guests joined us
for Christmas dinner.

I FOUND
insight in seeing things
from another angle.

When we make a conscious effort to look,
a new perspective is often
just around the corner.

I LOST
my yearly dollar gift
from my grandma
after she passed away.

I FOUND
I missed her a lot
more than the dollar.

*emories of special people are
worth far more than anything
we can fit in an envelope.*

I LOST
my composure in the midst of
my holiday piano recital.

I FOUND
how uncomfortable I could make
a basement full of people feel.

*No matter how hard others are
pulling for us, only we can
compose the proper outcome.*

I LOST
access to the box of chocolates
after being caught
tampering with them.

I FOUND
that poking holes to find the caramel ones
didn't make the coconut ones
go away.

Putting up with the bad can make the holiday season all the sweeter.

WE LOST
electricity and heat during
a holiday blizzard.

WE FOUND
that togetherness could generate
a different kind of power.

*Some of the warmest moments in life
are neither expected nor billed for.*

I LOST
my nerve to come home
for Christmas break when
I wasn't bearing gifts.

I FOUND
a mother with open arms
ready to accept me and my laundry.

Tolerance is a gift
for those who appreciate it . . .
not expect it.

I LOST
interest in singing with my fellow carolers
and I ran off between the houses.

I FOUND,
as the music faded,
so did the fun of my infraction.

Companionship is reserved for those who stay in tune with the Christmas spirit.

I LOST

feelings of suspense when
we opened gifts before going to church.

I FOUND

that, although the anticipation was gone,
the reasons to give thanks
were plentiful.

Taking time to give thanks
has an excitement all its own.

I LOST
my spirit when the Christmas season
wasn't making me happy.

I FOUND
that happiness doesn't come *to* me;
it comes *out of* me.

*Those who have difficulty going
within often go without . . .
happiness is an inside job.*

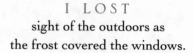

I LOST
sight of the outdoors as
the frost covered the windows.

I FOUND
the warm touch of another's hand
cleared the view.

*True friends help us
see the world differently.*

I LOST
the world's biggest snow fort to
a mid-December thaw.

I FOUND
that material things are temporary
but memories last a lifetime.

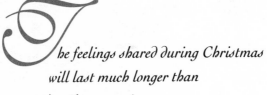

*he feelings shared during Christmas
will last much longer than
the gifts we receive.*

I LOST
count of the gifts my mom had given
to people outside our home.

I FOUND,
after seeing the number of gifts
she received, how her generosity
was richly rewarded.

Those with a heart of gold
will never have empty pockets.

I LOST
my gift-wrapping responsibilities
at the hardware store by
doing a sloppy job.

I FOUND
that, just because I wasn't
giving or receiving it,
each gift was still special.

*In the true spirit of Christmas,
we should put ourselves aside and
get wrapped up in the excitement of others.*

I LOST

my temper over some "crack" about
my Christmas haircut.

I FOUND

my reaction wasn't about my haircut
but something deeper
that needed to be addressed.

*In this emotionally charged season,
showing sensitivity to others
may be our greatest gift.*

I LOST
hope when all the gifts
under the tree had been opened
and I hadn't received the skis I wanted.

I FOUND
them in the garage
where my mom had sent me
to get a trash bag.

*Keep hope alive during a season
that can produce surprises at every turn.*

I LOST

the time to get out and do something
for less fortunate people
over the holidays.

I FOUND

that some things are easier
to *think about* than to
actually *do*.

Intent without effort makes no difference at all.

I LOST
sight of that big ol' stick
that measured our holiday snowfall amount.

I FOUND
I didn't realize how much snow
had accumulated until the stick was
out of sight.

*It is true with family and friends that
we don't see what we have
until they're gone.*

I LOST
my holiday zeal and decided against
decorating my house
for Christmas.

I FOUND
that, if I wasn't excited,
how could I expect my guests to be.

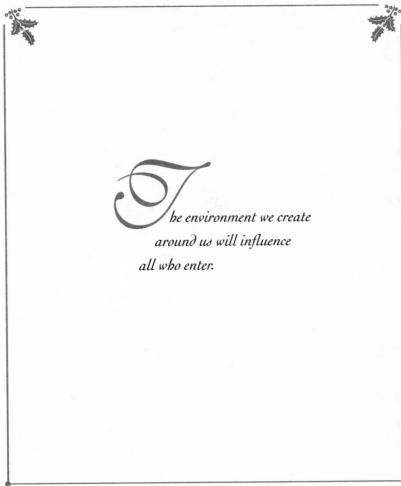

The environment we create around us will influence all who enter.

I LOST
interest in the same year-in
and year-out gift-giving routine.

I FOUND
that the ritual didn't need to change,
I did.

*The attitudes with which we
approach this season
will dictate our results
in the end.*

I LOST

understanding for the family
whose beliefs didn't include
the celebration of Christmas.

I FOUND

that some things aren't right or wrong . . .
just different.

*Christmas is about accepting
the convictions of others
as much as practicing our own faith.*

I LOST
credibility with a girlfriend
when I gave her the sweatpants
intended for my mom.

I FOUND
her lukewarm response
appropriate for my actions.

utting little thought into
an important gift is
never a good fit.

I LOST
track of the number of Christmas snacks
I had been putting into my body.

I FOUND
a soft gentle reminder around my waistline
as the holiday neared its end.

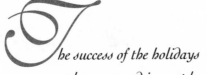

*he success of the holidays
can be measured in part by
the bathroom scale.*

I LOST
track of time recalling
many fond memories of Christmases past.

I FOUND
that reliving a peaceful past is
always time well spent.

Looking back at special moments brings simplicity to complicated times.

I LOST
my Christmas spirit when
I was honked at continually
in a busy parking lot.

I FOUND
I didn't have so much extra energy
that I could exhaust it on others.

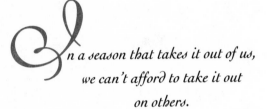

In a season that takes it out of us,
we can't afford to take it out
on others.

I LOST

the joy of visiting my great uncle John's farm
at Christmas once it was demolished.

I FOUND,

upon receiving a portrait of that home,
a permanent reminder of someone
in my life who was good.

*Hung in just the right spot,
a picture can cover a hole in the wall
and fill a hole in our hearts.*

I LOST
patience with the guy next to me
in church who couldn't sing
"Joy to the World"
to save his life.

I FOUND
he was there to
celebrate Christmas,
not to entertain me.

When looking for talent alone,
one's spirit is often overlooked.

I LOST
myself in thought
while staring into the
perfectly smooth ice.

I FOUND,
in my reflection,
a sense of clarity in
who I was.

*Seeking knowledge of self will
allow others to see us
for who we really are.*

I LOST
my excitement when I saw
the box under the wrapping paper
came from a cheap department store.

I FOUND
the importance of seeing what
was inside before casting judgment.

Giving people the opportunity to open up could very easily change a verdict.

I LOST
respect for the man who didn't
share my enthusiasm for
the Christmas holidays.

I FOUND
that, to some, holidays are
full of memories they want to forget.

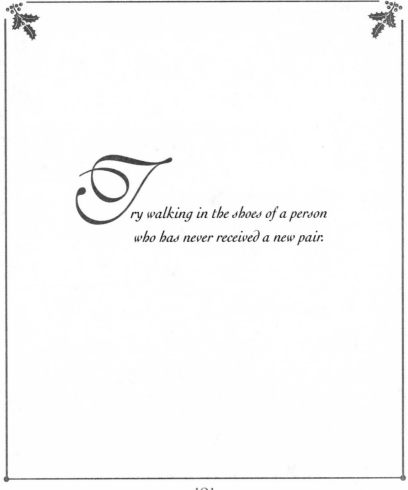

Try walking in the shoes of a person who has never received a new pair.

I LOST
the remote control to
my little nephew's new race car.

I FOUND
that, if the car didn't budge,
neither did he.

*oving people is a result of
knowing where their buttons are
and which ones to push.*

I LOST
my concern for saving
the pretty boxes and ribbons as
I tore into my gifts.

I FOUND,
a year later, a shortage of
—guess what—
boxes and ribbons when it came time to
do the wrapping.

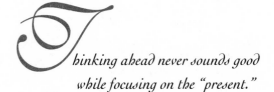

*Thinking ahead never sounds good
while focusing on the "present."*

I LOST
my opportunity to impress when
I forgot to bring my expensive wine
for Christmas dinner.

I FOUND
my mom's wine tasted
just as good.

*It's not what is served
but who serves it
that can make the difference.*

I LOST
what was once
a beautiful candle as
it slowly dripped away.

I FOUND,
when it had melted,
it had served its purpose well.

*If only we lived our lives with
the kind of purpose that still shines
after we've been extinguished.*

I LOST
the holiday pool tournament to
my dad as it came down to the last shot.

I FOUND

the enjoyment I got along the way
overshadowed my disappointment
in the end.

Perspective is finding victory in defeat.
Thankfully it only happened once.

I LOST
my composure when asked to
present the Christmas prayer
off the cuff.

I FOUND
it's hard to speak when
my heart is in my throat.

*Anything that comes from the heart will
eventually be heard loud and clear.*

I LOST
an opportunity to appreciate my mom
when I forgot to mention
her table decorations.

I FOUND
the importance of
acknowledging that which
often goes unnoticed.

*Gifts of time and creativity are
the ones we can't afford to overlook.*

I LOST
my fatigue after spending
most of the holiday season relaxing.

I FOUND
a resurgence of energy
that armed me for a new year.

W hen will we learn that having fresh batteries is an integral part of Christmas?

I LOST

my anticipation for Christmas
when I reached the age of responsibility.

I FOUND

I wasn't ready to make the shift from
receiver to provider.

Leadership in the family happens when you stop being consumed by hope . . . and begin to fulfill it for others.

I LOST
my courage to go anywhere
near the mistletoe while girls
were in the vicinity.

I FOUND,
in later years,
reasons to bring a few sprigs of mistletoe
wherever I went.

*Our fears of the past can
become our tools of the future.*

I LOST

that Christmas feeling when
our family traded the beautiful white snow
for the brown desert sand.

I FOUND

Christmas is not as much
about where we are,
but who we are with.

*Having a "white Christmas" is
more the result of perspective than proximity.*

I LOST
my favorite seat in church
to an overflow Christmas crowd of people
I'd never seen before.

I FOUND
the House of God takes
no reservations.

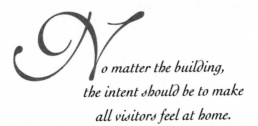

*No matter the building,
the intent should be to make
all visitors feel at home.*

I LOST
control of my emotions
during the singing of "Silent Night"
on Christmas Eve.

I FOUND
there are times when it's appropriate
to let down my guard.

*By being open to the Christmas spirit,
we allow it to strike familiar chords
every season.*

I LOST
the family connection
when I spent my first Christmas
away from home.

I FOUND
in my bride someone
who was willing to employ old customs
to enhance our new lives.

*By keeping traditions,
we realize the spirit of Christmas
will never die.*

I LOST

again at my effort to water
the Christmas tree sufficiently enough
to keep it alive.

I FOUND

that each passing tree
gives way to the birth of a new year.

What is so great about the Christmas season is that it ends with a fresh start.

I LOST
the radiance of our room
as the candles were extinguished
for the night.

I FOUND,
and kept, an afterglow
from another joyous holiday.

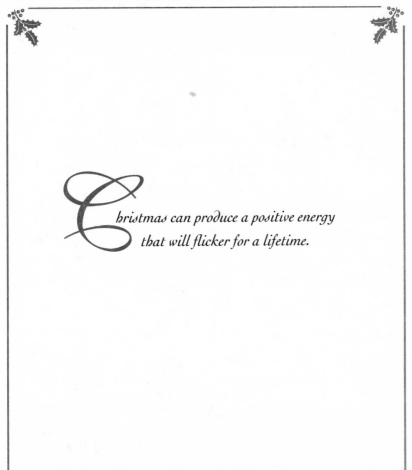

*Christmas can produce a positive energy
that will flicker for a lifetime.*

had a certain glow of anticipation as I awaited my dad's arrival from work. I knew his upcoming announcement would make me the envy of our class for the year ahead. So when I heard his car pull into the garage, I gathered our family in the kitchen for the confirmation of our Christmas trip to Florida.

"Well," my dad said as we all stood around him, "what I had hoped would be a big surprise has become a reality." He took a big pause for effect as he looked at each one of us.

"Today I was named Salesman of the Year!"

The kitchen erupted with joy, my brothers yelling, "Dad, that's great," and my mom saying, "I'm so proud of you," and me silently thinking, I don't think I'm going anywhere. I didn't say a word as I turned and walked into the living room. I only remember feeling empty in a room full of gifts.

Looking back, I realize that Christmas is about putting aside our own desires, and making time to celebrate and appreciate those people and events that make our lives possible.

So as the season approaches and there is so much to do,
It's time to remember it's not about you.

Your gift list is growing but your presents are few,
It's not going to matter, 'cause it's not about you.

You'll make everyone happy when Christmas is through
As long as you realize it's not about you.